How To Develop and
Implement Visual Supports

PRO-ED Series on Autism Spectrum Disorders

Edited by Richard L. Simpson

Titles in the Series

How To Develop
and
Implement
Visual Supports

Theresa L. Earles-Vollrath

Katherine Tapscott Cook

Jennifer B. Ganz

An International Publisher

8700 Shoal Creek Boulevard
Austin, Texas 78757-6897
800/897-3202   Fax 800/397-7633
www.proedinc.com

© 2006 by PRO-ED, Inc.
8700 Shoal Creek Boulevard
Austin, Texas 78757-6897
800/897-3202   Fax 800/397-7633
www.proedinc.com

Library of Congress Cataloging-in-Publication Data

How to write and implement social scripts / Jennifer B. Ganz ... [et al.].
        p. cm. — (PRO-ED series on autism spectrum disorders)
    Includes bibliographical references.
    ISBN 1-4164-0153-9 (softcover : alk. paper)
    1. Autistic children—education.   2. Social skills—Study and teaching.
I. Ganz, Jennifer B.   II. Series.
LC4717.5.H68 2006
371.94—dc22

                                                      2005019464

Art Director: Jason Crosier
Designer: Nancy McKinney-Point
This book is designed in Nexus Serif TF and Neutra Text.

Printed in the United States of America

4   5   6   7   8   9   10   11   21   20   19   18   17   16   15

Contents

Acknowledgments

The authors would like to thank the following individuals for sharing their work:

Judy Christiansen, Trails West State School, Kansas City, MO (Figure 2.2)

Linda La Pietra, Katherine Carpenter Elementary, Shawnee Mission School District, Shawnee Mission, KS (Figures 2.3, 3.3)

Judy Becker, Katherine Carpenter Elementary, Shawnee Mission School District, Shawnee Mission, KS (Figure 2.4)

Jennifer Savner Levinson, Shawnee Mission School District, Shawnee Mission, KS (Figures 2.6, 2.9, 3.4, 3.5, 3.6, 5.5)

Edna Smith, educational and behavioral consultant, Oasis for Teachers, Kansas City, MO (Figures 2.7, 3.7, 3.9, 3.15, 3.17, 5.6)

Laurie Koger, Communication Behavior Social Skills (CBSS) Program, Spring Branch Elementary, Independence School District, Independence, MO (Figures 2.7, 5.9, 5.10, 5.11)

Many figures use symbols from Mayer-Johnson:

Boardmaker, by Mayer-Johnson LLC. (1981–2004). The Picture Communications Symbols. All Rights Reserved Worldwide. Used with permission. Nonreproducible. (Figures 2.3, 2.4, 2.5, 2.6, 2.7, 2.8, 2.9, 2.10, 2.11, 3.1, 3.2, 3.3, 3.6, 3.7, 3.8, 3.9, 3.11, 3.12, 3.13, 3.14, 3.17, 3.18, 5.1, 5.2, 5.3, 5.4, 5.6, 5.9, 5.10, 5.11)

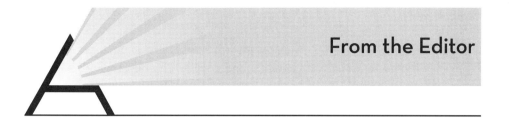

About Autism Spectrum Disorders

Autism spectrum disorders (ASD) are complex, neurologically based developmental disabilities that typically appear early in life. The Autism Society of America (2004) estimates that as many as 1.5 million people in the United States have autism or some form of pervasive developmental disorder. Indeed, its prevalence makes ASD an increasingly common and currently the fastest-growing developmental disability. ASD are perplexing and enigmatic. According to the *Diagnostic and Statistical Manual of Mental Disorders,* individuals with ASD have difficulty in interacting normally with others; exhibit speech, language, and communication difficulties (e.g., delayed speech, echolalia); insist on routines and environmental uniformity; engage in self-stimulatory and stereotypic behaviors; and respond atypically to sensory stimuli (American Psychiatric Association, 2000; Simpson & Myles, 1998). In some cases, aggressive and self-injurious behavior may be present in these individuals. Yet, in tandem with these characteristics, children with ASD often have normal patterns of physical growth and development, a wide range of cognitive and language capabilities, and some individuals with ASD have highly developed and unique abilities (Klin, Volkmar, & Sparrow, 2000). These widely varied characteristics necessitate specially designed interventions and strategies orchestrated by knowledgeable and skilled professionals.

Preface to the Series

Teaching and managing learners with ASD can be demanding, but favorable outcomes for children and youth with autism and autism-related disabilities depend on professionals using appropriate and valid methods in their education. Because identifying and correctly using effective teaching methods is often enormously challenging (National Research Council, 2001; Simpson et al., 2005), it is the intent of this series to provide professionals with scientifically based methods for intervention. Each book in the series is designed to assist professionals and parents in choosing and correctly using a variety of interventions that have the potential to produce significant benefits for children and youth with ASD. Written in a user-friendly, straightforward fashion by qualified and experienced professionals, the books are aimed at individuals who seek practical solutions and strategies for successfully working with learners with ASD.

Richard L. Simpson
Series Editor

References

American Psychiatric Association. (2000). *Diagnostic and statistical manual of mental disorders* (4th ed., text rev.). Washington, DC: Author.

Autism Society of America. (2004). *What is autism?* Retrieved March 11, 2005, from http://autism-society.org

Klin, A., Volkmar, F., & Sparrow, S. (2000). *Asperger syndrome.* New York: Guilford Press.

National Research Council. (2001). *Educating children with autism.* Committee on Educational Interventions for Children with Autism, Division of Behavioral and Social Sciences and Education. Washington, DC: National Academy Press.

Simpson, R., de Boer-Ott, S., Griswold, D., Myles, B., Byrd, S., Ganz, J., et al. (2005). *Autism spectrum disorders: Interventions and treatments for children and youth.* Thousand Oaks, CA: Corwin Press.

Simpson, R. L., & Myles, B. S. (1998). *Educating children and youth with autism: Strategies for effective practice.* Austin, TX: PRO-ED.

Visual schedules and other visual supports are essential components of programs for children with autism spectrum disorders (ASD). Visual supports can be used to provide information, to teach self-help skills, to teach independent work skills, to help students understand expectations, and many other ways. Additionally, visual supports can be used with all students regardless of their intellectual capacities or verbal abilities. In students with ASD, visual supports are highly effective with higher functioning students, such as those with Asperger Syndrome (AS), as well as more severely impaired students with classic forms of autism.

In typical teaching situations, teachers rely on students' auditory systems, such as when teaching via lectures. This poses a problem for students with ASD, who have difficulty attending to, modulating, and understanding auditory input. Additionally, these students' hypersensitivity to sounds and their inability to discriminate relevant sounds (e.g., the teacher's voice) from irrelevant sounds (e.g., fans, humming of classroom lights, motor of overhead projector, children playing outside, planes flying overhead) frequently affect their ability to attend, react, and respond appropriately.

Therefore, many students with ASD learn better when visual supports and visual modes of teaching are used. Indeed, autism experts (Carr, 1985; Hodgdon, 1995; Quill, 1995; Savner & Myles, 2000) and teachers agree that many students with ASD have visual interpretation skills that are far superior to their auditory capabilities. Temple Grandin (1995), in describing her experiences growing up with autism, said that

> Most people in the so-called normal world think in words, but thinking in language and words is alien to me. I think totally in pictures. Visual thinking is like playing different tapes in a videocassette recorder in my imagination ... So to access spoken information that I have heard in the past, I replay a video of the person talking to me. To retrieve facts, I have to read them off a visualized page of a book or "replay the video" of some previous event.... I have difficulties with long strings of verbal information. If directions from a gas station contain more than three steps I have to write them down. (pp. 34–35)

Another individual with autism, Donna Williams (1994), confirmed Grandin's need for verbal steps or directions to be presented visually.

Williams said she was unable to learn math until all math steps were visually represented in written form.

According to Savner and Myles (2000), "For many children seeing a visual support is like having a light bulb go on in their head—they finally see the light and understand what you have been saying" (p. 2). Indeed, visual strategies are educational supports that maximize the visual strengths of students with ASD.

This section describes the steps involved in creating visual supports for students with ASD.

Determine the Type of Visual Supports

The first step in implementing visual supports for a student with ASD is to determine the type of supports the student needs to be successful in school, home, and community settings. As discussed later in this booklet, a variety of visual supports may benefit students with ASD. While some students may be successful with only a few visual supports, others will require intensive visual support systems. The type and number of visual supports used should depend on the individual needs of the student.

Determine the Design of the Visual Supports

Once a teacher has chosen the types of support to use, he or she will then determine the design of the support system. There are several factors to consider in this step.

Symbol Representation

Objects, people, and events can be represented in a variety of ways, ranging from concrete symbols such as actual objects to more abstract symbols such as written words. The level of representation used in a visual support should be determined by a student's ability to understand the representation. For example, if a student can match objects to objects but cannot match pictures in any way, then his or her visual support would be designed around objects. Whenever possible, the most age-appropriate representation level should be used. To help students achieve more advanced symbol

1

recognition, teachers should pair a student's current level of symbol system with higher representation levels. For example, if a student is functioning at the object level, a photograph representing the designated activity might be paired with the object to introduce the higher level concept. Similarly, if a student is functioning at the photograph level, a drawing or icon can be paired with the photograph. When using any visual representation system, a teacher should pair the symbol with the written word. Some children with autism can become early sight-word readers, and pairing words with their symbols promotes literacy. Figure 1.1 lists the levels of visual representation from abstract to concrete.

Because determining the most appropriate symbol to use in a visual support is an important consideration, teachers should take the necessary time to make this decision. In addition, teachers should examine the level of visual representation being used when a visual support does not seem to be working with a student. Simply changing the symbol may increase the success of the support.

Size

A teacher must also consider the size of any visual support. A student's physical and visual abilities should be considered when determining the size of the visual support, including the size of the visual representation.

Location

The location of the support will depend in part on its type (e.g., visual schedule, minischedule, social story). Visual schedules may be fastened to students' desks or hung on the wall using tape, Velcro, or magnets. If the visual support needs to be portable, it can be attached to an O-ring or placed in a small photo album or fanny pack. Wherever the visual support is located, it must be easily accessible to the student.

Color

For some students, the use of color on visual supports may help them discriminate among symbols and may define their type or category (e.g., distinguish a visual schedule from a minischedule). The use of color should depend on the needs of each student. For some students, color may be useful, for others, it may distract from the content of the visual support or be an unnecessary prompt.

Heirarchy of Levels of Representation

Level	Type	Example
Highest	Icon of sign language	 (Finished)
	Written phrase or sentence	"It's time for recess."
	Word	"Recess"
	Icon (black-and-white line drawing)	 (Computer)
	Colored drawing	Same as the icon above but in color
	Photograph	Photograph can be general such as a photo of a "work area" or more specific such as a photo of the materials used to complete the task or of the student completing the task.
	Miniature object	Small version of the object used in the activity (e.g., toilet from a dollhouse used to represent bathroom)
	Full-sized object	Actual object used in the activity (e.g., a spoon used to represent lunchtime)
Lowest	Physical gesture	A pointing gesture to the reading area indicates that it is time for reading

FIGURE 1.1. Hierachy of levels of representation.

Gather the Symbols

The third step in developing a visual support is to gather the needed symbols, including obtaining objects, taking pictures, making icons or another type of drawing, and so forth. If miniature objects are the symbol of choice, refrigerator magnets, dollhouse furnishings, doll toys, and plastic foods can be used. If icons are chosen, Mayer-Johnson (www.mayer-johnson.com) offers a computer program that contains thousands of Picture Communication Symbols (PCS) in either color or black and white. The symbols can be made any size and can carry various labels or messages. In addition, Web sites such as www.do2learn.com and www.tinsnips.org contain many printable icons. When choosing icons or line drawings, teachers should carefully determine whether to use color or black and white. As mentioned previously, some children with ASD may focus on the colors in the icon rather than the entire picture. Using black-and-white icons tends to alleviate this problem. If the visual support uses photographs, there are several ways to get digital photos. A teacher could take the photos needed with a digital camera. Figure 1.2 contains suggestions by Hodgdon (1995) for taking pictures to be used in visual supports. In addition, computer software such as Picture This and Flash and Web sites such as http://www.tinsnips.org and http://trainland.tripod.com/pecs.htm contain printable digital images.

Create the Visual Supports

Once the teacher has gathered the symbols that will be used in the visual supports, he or she will be ready for the final steps in creating the supports, including the following:

- **Laminate the visual support or cover it in clear contact paper.**
  This will ensure durability. Vinyl envelope covers, photo album page covers, and baseball card covers can also be used to prevent damage.
- **Make multiple copies of the visual support or its symbols.** This practice will prevent you from needing to re-create the support if it should wear out, get lost, or otherwise be unavailable. Store extra copies of the visual support or its symbols in an alphabetically divided index-card box, a three-ring binder containing pages with Velcro attached, slide-projector pages, or in the small drawers of fishing tackle boxes or thread storage containers (Frost & Bondy, 2002).

Picture-Taking Guidelines

- **Identify the critical element.** Determine the exact element that will provide the student with the relevant information needed to better understand the situation. This could be a close-up picture of an object, a picture of the student completing the desired activity, and so forth.

- **Shoot close up.** Shooting close up will ensure that the critical element is the essential part of the picture and is easily identifiable to the student. You will need to become familiar with the focus limits of your camera when shooting close up.

- **Eliminate the background.** Too much background will distract the student from the critical element. Taking pictures against plain backgrounds will help the student focus on the critical element. Suggestions include placing objects on poster board, not on textured carpet, and taking pictures of people standing against a bare wall, rather than in front of a bulletin board full of artwork.

- **Watch the lighting.** When taking photos indoors, a flash will probably be needed. Therefore, you will need to learn the distance limits for your camera's flash. Using a flash while standing too close to an object can cause the photo to appear washed out, whereas not using a flash when needed can make the photo appear dark. Similarly, direct sunlight from windows will affect the lighting in the photo. When outdoors, do not take photos when you are facing directly into the sun or when the sun is shining directly on the subject.

- **Take generic photos when possible.** While some students will require personalized visual supports, other students may be able to understand and successfully use systems containing more generic photos. For example, instead of taking a photo of each student setting the table, take one photo that shows a pair of hands setting the table. Using generic photos when possible will decrease the amount of time that it takes to develop the visuals because one picture could be printed several times.

FIGURE 1.2. Guidelines for taking pictures to be used in visual supports. *Note.* Adapted from *Visual Strategies for Improving Communication: Practical Supports for School and Home,* by L. A. Hodgdon, 1995, Troy, MI: QuirkRoberts.

- **Standardize your Velcro.** To ensure that icons can be used with multiple supports such as visual schedules and minischedules, you should consistently attach either the loop side or the fuzzy side of the Velcro to the icon. All icons will then be interchangeable and any replacement icons will fit easily into the system.
- **Do not spend an excessive amount of time up front making the system perfect.** The visual support system may need to be revised several times until it works well for the student. The system can be made more permanent once it is finalized.

Other considerations are specific to the type of visual support system being designed and are discussed in later sections of this booklet.

A variety of visual supports are discussed in forthcoming sections, including support systems in the following categories: (a) visual supports that provide information, (b) visual strategies that support behavior, (c) visual supports that structure the learning environment, (d) visuals that enhance communication, (e) visual supports that support social skill development, and (f) visual strategies that support calendar or other morning group activities.

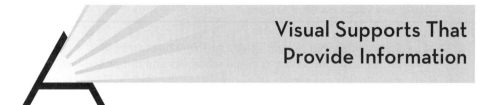

This section describes several types of visual supports that can be used to convey information to a student, including visual schedules, minischedules, task organizers, calendars, and memory aids.

Visual Schedules

Visual schedules give students an overview of each day's activities and events by connecting tasks with the specific times at which they occur. This process provides myriad benefits for students with ASD. First, visual schedules present the abstract concept of time in a concrete and manageable form. Many students with ASD find the concept of time difficult to understand, which may lead to stress, anxiety, and frustration because they are unable to determine when preferred activities may occur, how activities are sequenced, or when nonpreferred activities may end. Accordingly, increasing students' abilities to predict daily events often can reduce stress. Another benefit of visual schedules is that they help teach students the concepts of change and flexibility. Visual schedules can also be used to stimulate communicative exchanges by discussing past, present, and future events (Twachtman, 1995). That is, visual schedules provide students with a means for requesting specific activities (e.g., lunch), asking when an activity will occur (e.g., go home, swing), and answering questions regarding their day (e.g., "What's next?") (Downing & Peckham-Hardin, 2001). Visual schedules can be used to increase on-task behavior and enhance students' abilities to transition independently from one activity to another (MacDuff, Krantz, & McClannahan, 1993). Another benefit of visual schedules is that they capitalize on the visual strengths of many students with ASD. Finally, the permanence of visual schedules, as opposed to the transience of speech, allows students with ASD to refer to their schedules as often as needed to understand expectations and temporal relationships and sequences.

Constructing a Visual Schedule

The instructions for consulting a visual schedule are as follows:

- Decide if the schedule will be a group schedule or an individual schedule. Although some students with ASD are able to understand and use a group schedule, many will require individual schedules that will address their specific needs.
- Determine the activities that will be occurring throughout the student's day.
- Determine the appropriate level of visual representation, using the previously described guidelines.
- Determine format and arrangement. The visual schedule can be arranged using a top-to-bottom or left-to-right format. In addition, a visual schedule can be placed in a three-ring binder, a small photo album, or a manila or pocket folder. Other arrangements include placing a visual schedule on a clipboard or a dry-erase board, taping it to a desk, or using Velcro to affix it to a desk or a wall. A major consideration when determining visual schedule format and arrangement is portability. Some students may need to carry their visual schedules or individual symbols from the schedule as they transition within their classrooms and schools. Carrying the visual schedule or portion of the schedule can also assist students who are easily distracted or who become overstimulated during transitions by reminding them of the upcoming event as well as its location.
- Establish a "finished" indicator. A finished indicator is a student's way of signaling the end of an activity. The finished indicator also allows a student to interact with the schedule and assists him or her in understanding that activities are changing and seeing that the number of remaining activities is decreasing as the day progresses. There are a variety of finished indicator options, including removing symbols and placing them in a "finished" or "all done" pocket or tub as they are completed, turning symbols over, crossing off the activity with a dry-erase marker, drawing a line through completed tasks, and checking off a box upon successful completion of an activity.
- Decide how much information the student can handle at one time. Can the student view the schedule for the entire day or does the schedule need to be divided into smaller increments (e.g., a morning schedule and an afternoon schedule)? Visual schedules that provide information can also be reduced to a first–next type of schedule on which only two symbols are placed at one time. At least two symbols should be visible at any one time because the purpose of the visual schedule is to assist students in understanding that activities occur sequentially, not in isolation.
- Determine if the student will be involved in the daily construction of his or her visual schedule. This involvement may vary from having the student place the symbols in the correct order on the schedule either

by memory or by looking at an exact duplicate of the schedule, watch the teacher complete the schedule, or copy the schedule onto paper. The level of participation will depend on the skills of the student.

• Determine what opportunities exist for choice within the visual schedule. Can the student determine the order in which certain activities are completed? Can the student select between several activities?

• Establish a schedule routine. There are several options for this step. Hodgdon (1995) recommended developing a verbal routine to guide students in using their schedules. For this option, the teacher selects a verbal phrase that serves as a prompt for students to check their schedules (e.g., "check schedule"). A second option is to use a visual cue. Visual cues should be given to students during transitions and indicate to them that they need to check their schedules to determine upcoming activities. Examples of "check schedule" visual cues include a laminated index card on which the student's name is written, a poker chip, or a popsicle stick. An advantage of using a visual cue over a verbal prompt is that visual cues promote independence more rapidly than most verbal prompts. Examples of visual supports that provide information are shown in Figures 2.1 through 2.4.

Teaching Students To Use Visual Schedules

Unfortunately, many teachers who use visual schedules fail to systematically teach their students to use the support system. Although there is no single best way to teach the use of visual support systems, the following steps can serve as a general guide. Students may initially require prompts to participate in these steps.

- Take students to their visual schedules regularly as a means of developing a "check schedule" routine.
- Assist students in pointing to the first object/photo/icon/word on their schedules.

FIGURE 2.1. Object schedule in which actual objects represent upcoming activities and pages are turned to represent the completion of an activity.

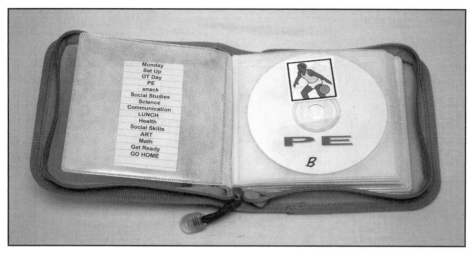

FIGURE 2.2. Visual schedule for an older student with ASD in which old compact discs are placed in a CD holder.

- Assist students in moving to the identified area or activity as indicated on their schedules.
- Have students complete the activity noted on their schedules.
- Direct students back to their schedules. A verbal script such as "Math is finished, check your schedule" can be used in this step.
- Assist students in returning to their schedules to identify and complete the next activity using the previously described steps.

Special Considerations
- Note that physical prompts may be necessary initially. However, the level of prompting should be faded as soon as acquisition is accomplished because the goals for students who use visual supports are to gain independence and lessen prompt dependence.
- Encourage verbal students to verbalize each step shown on their visual schedules. Repeating the verbal scripts correlated with their routines may become a self-talk or self-prompt strategy that will assist students in regulating their own behavior (Hodgdon, 1995).

Minischedules

Minischedules are often considered to be the second step in the hierarchy of visual supports for students with ASD and other developmental disabilities. Whereas visual schedules provide students with a general overview of

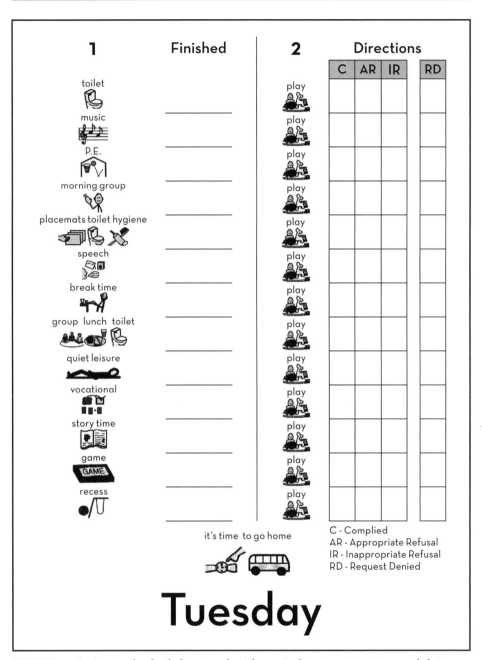

FIGURE 2.3. A visual schedule paired with a reinforcement system and data collection. When each activity is completed, the student places a checkmark in the Finished column. On the right, the teacher records data on the student's compliance: C = Complied, AR = Appropriate Refusal, IR = Inappropriate Refusal, RD = Request Denied.

FIGURE 2.4. Group visual schedule using icons paired with photos. As each activity is completed, the teacher turns the card around.

the day's activities, minischedules provide greater structure by describing the exact activities that will occur during a designated time period. For example, if a visual schedule indicates that it is time for reading, the corresponding minischedule indicates, sequentially, the specific activities that will occur during reading time (e.g., review sight words, read story, complete worksheet). Thus, minischedules can supplement visual schedules by providing greater detail. In addition, the increased level of detail provided in minischedules helps facilitate independent work behaviors (Hodgdon, 1995) for some students with ASD.

Minischedules are constructed using steps similar to those used for visual schedules:

- Determine the specific activities that will occur during each designated subject. For example, if the subject is P.E., then the activities that occur may include warming up, running laps, playing basketball, getting a drink, going back to class, and so forth.
- Determine the appropriate level of visual representation, using the previously described guidelines.
- Determine format and arrangement. The minischedule can be arranged using a top-to-bottom or left-to-right format. In addition, a minischedule can be placed in a three-ring binder, a small photo album, or a manila or pocket folder. It may be helpful if the minischedule is formatted and arranged in the same way as the visual schedule. Depending on the needs of the individual student, however, it may not be a necessity.
- Place the same symbol used in the visual schedule on the minischedule. Using the same symbol on the minischedule will help the student correlate the activities listed in the minischedule with the task or subject listed in the visual schedule.
- Establish the "finished" indicator. As previously noted, there are a variety of finished indicators, such as removing the symbol and placing it in a "finished" or "all done" pocket or tub, placing a token or chip on the picture representing the completed task, placing an icon depicting the symbol for "finished" on the picture representing the completed task, turning the symbol over, crossing off the activity with a dry-erase marker, drawing a line through the task, and checking off a box.
- Decide how much information the student can consume at any one time. Can the student view all of the activities listed in the minischedule or does it need to be broken into smaller increments? The schedule can be reduced as far as to a first–next type of schedule on which only two symbols are placed at one time.
- Determine the opportunities for choice within the minischedule. Assessing whether a student can determine the order in which certain activities are completed and whether a student can select between several activities are key elements in this step.

An example of a minischedule is shown in Figure 2.5. Teachers should use the guidelines already presented for visual schedules to create minischedules.

FIGURE 2.5. Minischedule for transitioning during center time.

Task Organizers

A third type of visual support system that provides information is the task organizer. This type of support augments minischedules by breaking down the exact steps associated with completing each of the activities listed in a student's minischedule. For example, if the minischedule indicates "complete worksheet," the task organizer will provide words or symbols representing the steps associated with completing the worksheet (e.g., get worksheet, get pencil, put name on worksheet, complete worksheet, review answers, place worksheet in finish basket). Therefore, task organizers assist students in being maximally independent in completing tasks. Task organizers are also useful for teaching adaptive or self-care skills, such as those required for taking a shower, getting dressed, making popcorn, and so forth. Indeed, "task organizers work for any activity that requires several steps to complete a task" (Hodgdon, 1995, p. 79).

Constructing Task Organizers

• List any materials that the student may need to complete the identified task (Hodgdon, 1995).
• Task-analyze the steps needed to complete a given task. For example, if the "cooking" minischedule indicates that it is time to make popcorn, the task organizer may contain the following steps: "go to cabinet, open cabinet door, get popcorn, close cabinet door, go to microwave, open microwave door, place popcorn bag in microwave, shut microwave door, press the popcorn button, wait, when timer sounds open microwave door, remove popcorn, return to table." Task organizers also can be used to show a student common daily routines such as arriving at school (e.g., hang up backpack, select lunch, bell work), going through the lunch line (e.g., stand in line; get

tray; get spoon, fork, straw, and napkin; place spoon, fork, straw, napkin on tray; select a meat; select a vegetable). When determining the required steps, it may be helpful to walk through the task yourself or observe a same-aged peer completing the task while you record the steps. A task organizer can include as much or as little detail as necessary for a student to successfully and independently complete a specified task.

• Determine the order in which the steps should be completed. Some activities will need to be completed sequentially, whereas others can be completed in a more flexible manner.

• Determine the appropriate level of visual representation, using the previously described guidelines.

• Determine the task organizer's format and arrangement. Task organizers can be arranged in a top-to-bottom or left-to-right format and placed on a sentence strip, in a three-ring binder, or in a manila folder.

• Select a location for the task organizer. Should the task organizer be placed in a permanent place such as on the wall or table or should it be portable?

• Establish the "finished" indicator. As previously noted, finished indicators can take a variety of forms: removing the symbol and placing it in a "finished" or "all done" pocket or tub, turning the symbol over, crossing off the activity with a dry-erase marker, drawing a line through the task, or checking off a box.

Teaching Students To Use Their Task Organizers

Students must be taught how to use task organizers. Hodgdon (1995) recommended the following steps:

• Direct student's attention to the task organizer.

• Verbally recite the script associated with each step depicted in the task organizer without adding any verbal prompts.

• If further prompting is necessary, use gestures (i.e., point to each symbol), modeling (i.e., demonstrate the step), or physical prompts (i.e., take the student's hand and assist him or her in completing the step). If verbal prompts are necessary, they should be faded as quickly as possible. A primary reason for implementing task organizers is to assist students in becoming more independent. Thus, continual use of verbal prompts may inhibit independence.

• Encourage verbal students to verbalize each step as it is completed. Repeating verbal scripts may become a successful self-talk or self-prompt strategy for behavioral self-regulation.

• Guide students' attention to their task organizers after each activity step is completed and assist them in understanding how to move to the next step (e.g., turn the page, point to the symbol representing the next step).

15

- Ensure that all prompts, verbal and physical, are faded.
- Reduce the number of steps in the task organizer as needed. Once students learn to complete the tasks, they may no longer need a fully detailed list of visual cues.

Note that minischedules and task organizers should be used only when students need extra structure to understand activities or to provide opportunities for choice and decision making. These tools can be applied in layers, therein encouraging students to function at their most appropriate level of independence. For example, some students require minimal external structure and need only a daily schedule. But others need more assistance to complete tasks on their daily schedules and often benefit from a series of minischedules for each major activity depicted on their daily schedule. Finally, for students who need maximum structure to work independently, a combination of daily schedules, minischedules, and task organizers will best meet their needs. Examples of task organizers are provided in Figures 2.6 and 2.7.

Calendars

Calendars are visual supports that assist students in understanding the concept of time relative to organizing their lives and understanding sequences of activities. Calendars can provide information on a variety of topics, such as school days versus weekends or holidays, doctor or therapy appointments, the day when a brother will be coming home from college, and school field trips. Students can be taught to refer to their calendars daily and to mark off each day as it occurs. Crossing off the days as they occur often permits students to view or count the days until special target activities occur. Figures 2.8 and 2.9 provide examples of calendars.

FIGURE 2.6. One page of a task organizer for making a sandwich.

Play with Baby Doll

 Rock the baby.

"Rock-a-bye baby."

 Give the baby a bottle.

"Here's your bottle, baby."

 Feed the baby.

"Eat your lunch, baby."

 Hug the baby.

"Nice baby."

 Give the baby her pacifier.

"Here's your pacifier, baby."

 Put the baby to bed.

"Night, night, baby."

Clean up time.

FIGURE 2.7. Task organizer that teaches appropriate play behavior with a doll. *Note.* The words in quotation marks indicate the verbal script for the student.

FIGURE 2.8. Calendar visual support showing the return of a family member(s).

FIGURE 2.9. Specific icons are added to each day for this calendar.

Memory Aids

Because many students with ASD appear unorganized and forgetful, and frequently forget needed materials such as books, supplies, and clothing items, teachers should provide methods to assist students in remembering various items. This will further promote maximum independence in the students. Visual memory aids are such a support. In this support, the materials needed for a given situation (e.g., school items such as backpack, math book, calculator) are specified. Memory aids frequently appear as checklists

18

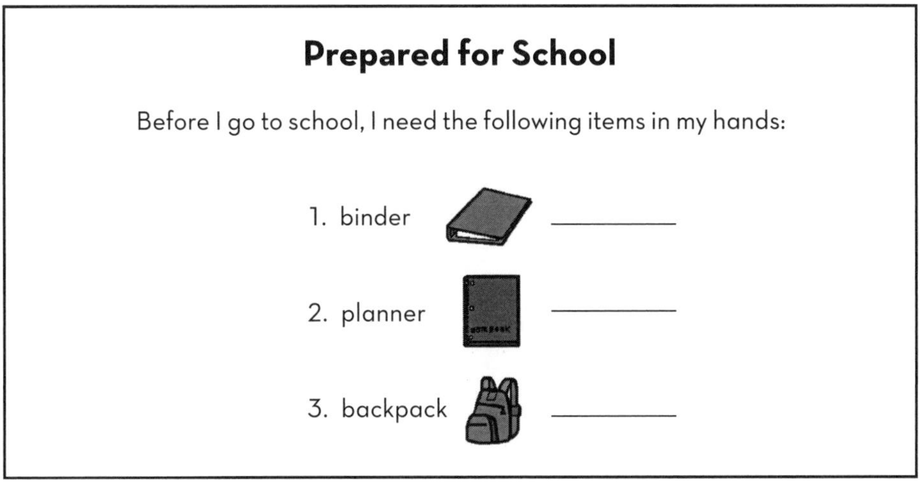

Prepared for School

Before I go to school, I need the following items in my hands:

1. binder _____

2. planner _____

3. backpack _____

FIGURE 2.10. Checklist of materials needed for school, used as a memory aid.

Flush the Toilet

that are posted in strategic areas, such as in a student's locker, to remind him or her of needed materials for specific classes or for home. Figures 2.10 and 2.11 provide examples of memory aids.

FIGURE 2.11. Memory aids provide visual reminders for self-help behaviors and must be used in the corresponding location. This memory aid would be placed above the toilet or on the inside of the bathroom door.

19

This section reviews visual strategies that support students' behavior.

Turn-Taking Cards

Turn taking is a difficult concept for any child to understand, but it is particularly difficult for children with ASD. To be able to take turns, one must be aware of the social implications of waiting one's turn (e.g., others will like me and want to play with me) and understand the concept of "waiting." These concepts can be made more meaningful through the use of a visual support. For example, a card with a symbol representing "My turn" or the words "My turn" can be placed on the card. The card can be passed from student to student as each takes his or her turn. This type of visual strategy can also facilitate verbal responses. For example, after a student with ASD completes his or her turn, he or she could hand the card to another student while simultaneously saying, "Your turn."

Waiting Symbols

Waiting is a difficult skill for many children to learn. For students with ASD, waiting frequently presents problems because of an inability to delay gratification and a difficulty in understanding the concept of waiting. Such students will require specific instruction to learn appropriate waiting behaviors. Visual supports can be used to teach these skills. For example, a child can be given a symbol representing "wait" to hold during a wait period. This can be paired with physical supports, such as placing chairs near a waiting area and setting a timer.

Before he or she is able to understand "wait" and successfully use the corresponding visual support, the student must first learn how to use the support tool. This instruction should initially occur in a structured setting where the adult can control access to the reinforcer and the time the student must wait (Frost & Bondy, 2002). For example, a teacher would not want to attempt to teach a "wait" lesson in a line at a fast-food restaurant because he or she would be unable to control reinforcers or the wait time (Frost & Bondy, 2002). Rather, this skill would best be taught in a classroom while the student is waiting his or her turn on a platform swing, for example. Frost and Bondy (2002) recommended the following steps for teaching a student to wait:

Step 1: Waiting less than 30 seconds

- Give the student his or her visual (e.g., card with symbol representing "wait" or a Formica chip with the word "wait"). Initially the wait card may provide the student with something to do while waiting (e.g., hold the card, look at the card); however, over time it should "serve as a promissory note—the student learns that as long as he holds it, good things are sure to follow" (p. 259).
- Arrange lessons wherein a student requests a desired item. When the student requests the item, hand him or her the wait card and say, "Wait." Within 2 to 3 seconds, take the wait card from the student while simultaneously saying, "Nice waiting!" and then give the requested item. It is important that the initial wait periods are short to ensure student success.
- Continue this training across different requests and environments.
- Gradually increase the wait periods by 1 or 2 seconds.
- If the student demonstrates inappropriate behaviors during the wait period, then the interval is too long. Gently take the wait card from the student and end the lesson by redirecting the student to another task without giving the requested item. Attempt the wait lesson at a later time, however, with a shorter interval.
- Intersperse opportunities to practice waiting across the day rather than conducting them all at once. Continue to grant requests to reinforce the act of requesting and to ensure that the student does not become frustrated.

Step 2: Waiting for periods longer than 30 seconds

- Gather materials to put in a "wait box," which should contain materials that the student can hold or interact with while waiting.
- Once the student has demonstrated success at waiting for 30 seconds, he or she is ready to move to the next step. At this time, when you direct a student to "wait," give him or her the wait card and something to do to occupy him or her. The student may select an item from the wait box for this purpose.
- Continue this practice over time while gradually increasing the time the student is expected to wait. Increase the wait interval to 1 minute, 2 minutes, 3 minutes, and so forth. When determining

the length of the interval, consider the student's age, cognitive and language abilities, and so forth.

- If a student is waiting for a particular material or activity, it may be beneficial to place a symbol representing the material or activity on the wait card. This added cue will assist the student in remembering why he or she is waiting and may assist in self-regulation of behavior to gain access to the desired item.
- As the wait period increases past 1 minute, it may be beneficial to add visual cues to assist the student in tracking the wait time. A Velcro dot can be placed on wait cards and the student can be given a star, happy face, or other item to attach to the Velcro. To begin this strategy, Frost and Bondy (2002) recommended placing one piece of Velcro on the wait card. Just as the wait period is about to end, give the student a star (with Velcro attached) and guide him or her in placing the star on the wait card. Then point to the wait card and say, "We're done waiting! Here's your _____." Over time, add a second Velcro dot and give the student the first star after approximately three fourths of the wait interval has elapsed. Wait a few seconds and then give the student the final star. As the student places the final star on the Velcro, point to the wait card while saying, "We're done waiting! Here's your _____." Continue to gradually increase the number of Velcro pieces on the wait card from two to three to four and then to five pieces. Figures 3.1 and 3.2 show examples of wait cards.
- Never say "Wait" to a student if you actually mean "No."

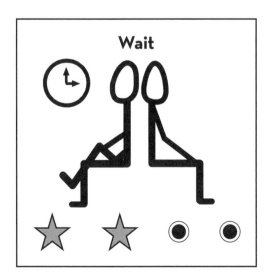

FIGURE 3.1. An example of a wait card in which stars are attached to Velcro dots as time passes.

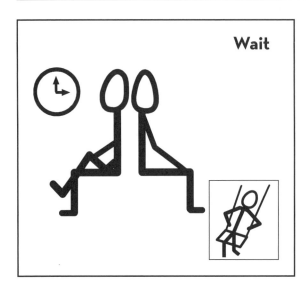

FIGURE 3.2. A wait card can be paired with the symbol for a desired reinforcer (e.g., swing) to increase the chance of success.

Remember: If the student "fails" a wait lesson, do not reinforce the failure by giving the student the item that he or she requested. Instead, change activities and try again later using a shorter interval.

Step 3: Waiting in the "real" world
- Over time, transition the wait system to the community where you cannot control the wait interval.
- When going out in the community to practice, take the wait card, the stars, and materials that will occupy the student while he or she waits.
- Begin in an environment where you can be sure that the wait period will be relatively short. For example, go to a fast-food restaurant at 2:00 in the afternoon, after the lunch crowd is gone.
- Provide the student with opportunities to wait in a variety of locations and settings.

Making Choices

Making choices is another area that can be addressed successfully through the use of visuals. Providing opportunities for students to make choices is a proactive means of addressing many challenging behaviors. As previously stated, students with ASD often rely on their visual abilities to facilitate comprehension of tasks or directions. Thus, by making choice-making opportunities visual, students will often be able to participate more successfully. Choice-making opportunities assist students with (a) increased attention, (b) improved communicative intent, (c) increased identification of their true wants or needs, (d) increased vocabulary, (e) decreased behavior problems, and (f) increased distraction from potential problems (Hodgdon, 1999).

Hodgdon (1999) specified five steps for facilitating visual-support-based choice making: (a) select several visuals that could be presented to the student as choices; (b) begin by presenting two choices; (c) encourage the child to indicate his or her choice; (d) give the student what he or she chose; and (e) move or remove the item not chosen to assist the student in understanding that he or she does not get what he or she did not request. Remember that making choices is essential for enhancing students' self-esteem and self-worth; thus, it must be embedded throughout their day. There are endless choices a student could make, including the order of activities listed on a visual schedule, writing utensil to use, work table to sit at, food to eat at lunch, friends to sit near, CDs to listen to, and so forth.

Visual supports that provide choice-making opportunities are frequently called choice boards. Choice boards display objects, pictures, icons, or words that represent a menu of choices, such as activities or reinforcers. Such boards can be constructed using poster board or any surface to which objects or icons can be attached. Velcro provides an excellent medium for adhering materials to a choice board and allows flexibility and ease for moving or switching objects.

Choice boards can be placed next to a student's daily schedule. When a designated choice time or break time arrives, the student can select a preferred activity from the board. Additionally, choice boards displaying preferred activities can be placed near free-time or break-time areas of rooms, providing a stimulus for independent selection of activities.

To make the choice board portable and to free wall space, a teacher could place pictures, icons, or words that represent available choices inside a three-ring binder or attach them to a clipboard. Figures 3.3 and 3.4 provide examples of choice-making supports.

Rules and Alternate Behaviors

When students engage in aberrant behavior, it is generally believed to be purposeful or self-regulated. Indeed, behavior is the number-one form of communication. More often than not, a student's deviance or "bad" behavior is only his or her attempt to communicate wants or needs. Visual supports can assist students with ASD not only in understanding behavioral expectations, but also in learning how to behave. Within this framework,

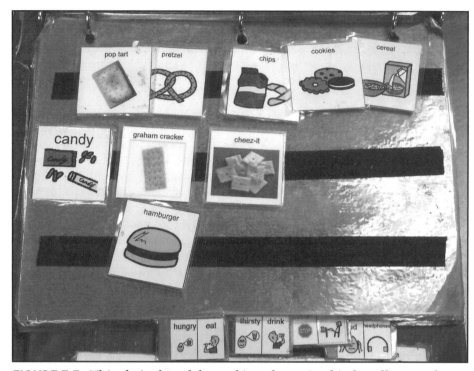

FIGURE 3.3. This choice board, housed in a three-ring binder, allows students to choose from a variety of food, drink, leisure, and break time activities, which are separated by category in the binder.

FIGURE 3.4. This choice board displays actual edibles, which is beneficial for students who need object representations. A material called Pour On is applied over the objects to ensure durability for multiple uses.

visual rules (a) tell students what to do and what not to do and (b) define consequences of breaking rules or engaging in aberrant behaviors (Hodgdon, 1999). Due to their social communication deficits, students with ASD are often unable to change their own behavior independently, often because they do not realize there is a need to change, do not know how to change, and do not recognize desired alternative behaviors. Many times aberrant behaviors occur because students are not taught alternative responses. Also, because rules are frequently not communicated clearly and expectations are not defined or consistently followed, it is difficult for students to behave as expected (Hodgdon, 1999).

For teachers who are designing rules and behavior guides, Hodgdon (1999) provided a succinct framework: (a) evaluate the situation from the student's perspective, (b) be specific and visual, (c) include only the most pertinent information and prioritize behavioral needs, (d) make visual supports logical and sequential, and (e) modify the visual rules or behavioral guide as necessary. Figures 3.5 through 3.8 provide examples of visual supports for defining rules and teaching alternate behaviors.

Consequence Maps

Predicting behavioral consequences can be particularly difficult for many children and adults with ASD. One of the difficulties in predicting consequences is that a behavior demonstrated in one setting with one individual

FIGURE 3.5. A student can wear this visual support on a belt loop or attach it to a binder ring.

27

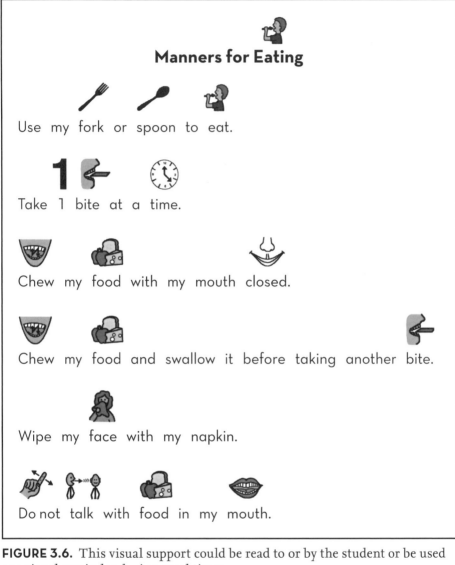

FIGURE 3.6. This visual support could be read to or by the student or be used as a visual reminder during meal times.

can have different consequences when exhibited in a different setting with a different person. Thus, consequences are affected by many factors such as the setting, individuals present, extremeness of the behavior, and world events (e.g., the terrorist attacks of Sept. 11, 2001). In addition, one must be able to look into the future and determine how one's behavior may affect

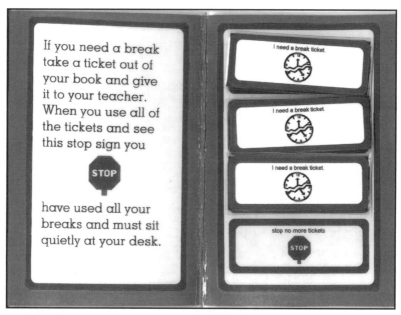

FIGURE 3.7. This system allows the student to request break tickets, which are attached with Velcro for easy removal.

others. Visual supports can be used to assist students in considering the different consequences of their behaviors and in selecting a behavior that will lead to a desired outcome. Figures 3.9 and 3.10 provide examples of consequence maps.

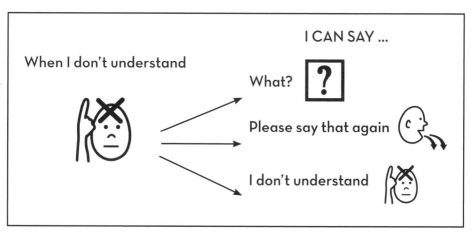

FIGURE 3.8. This visual support provides three behavior options for a student.

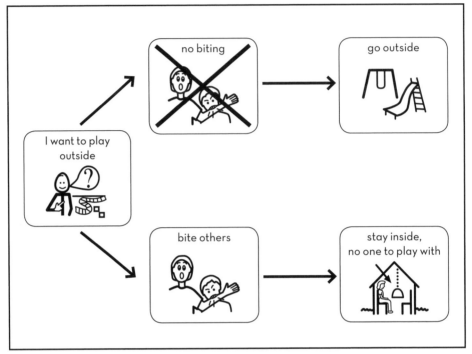

FIGURE 3.9. This visual outlines appropriate versus inappropriate behaviors and their corresponding consequences.

Calming Supports

Students with ASD who experience heightened levels of stress will frequently benefit from higher levels of visual support that capitalize on their visual skills and minimize reliance on auditory information. Calming supports also can be used to provide visual cues to guide students through debriefing periods, provide options to relieve stress, and present appropriate ways to deal with stressful situations that often lead to behavioral meltdowns. Figures 3.11 and 3.12 present examples of calming supports.

Indicating "No" and Behavioral Expectations

"No," "not right now," or "not appropriate" are difficult concepts for many children with ASD. It can be very confusing when, for example, students are

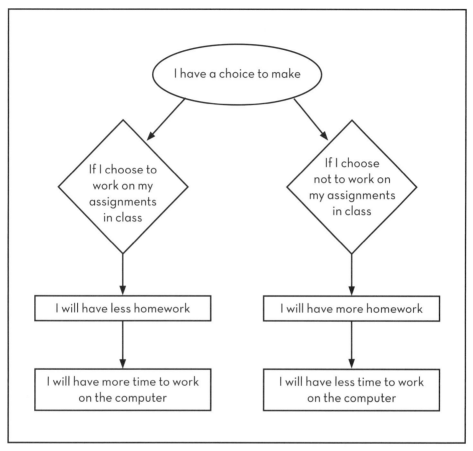

FIGURE 3.10. This consequence map shows consequences of a student's off-task behavior during class.

allowed to use the computer during some periods of the day but not others, or when they can sit in the beanbag during break time but not work time. One way to assist students in understanding these concepts is to represent them visually using the universal sign for "no" (i.e., a red circle with a line drawn through it). For example, a "no" symbol can be placed on a computer during times when it is not an option, then be removed when it is allowed. A "no" symbol can be placed on a beanbag chair during times when it would not be appropriate for a student to use (e.g., work time), then removed to allow the chair's use. In addition, a "no" symbol can be drawn onto a laminated symbol using a red dry-erase marker when a student requests an item that is not an available choice or when there is a change in the daily schedule and the selected activity is no longer scheduled to occur. Or, the universal sign for "no" can be copied or drawn onto paper or onto a transparency and

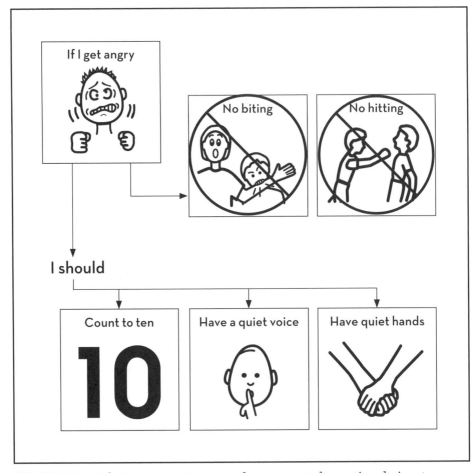

FIGURE 3.11. Calming supports are used to support alternative choices to inappropriate behavior sequences.

then taped or affixed to an item using Velcro. The symbol can be placed on the item at times when it is not an option. Figure 3.13 provides an example of how to indicate "no."

Visual supports can also assist students in understanding behavioral expectations. It can be difficult for students to comprehend why it is okay to run outside but not inside or why they can chase each other in the gym but not in their classroom. Although it is important to communicate expectations using positive statements, some students may also need a description of what not to do. Figure 3.14 provides an example of pairing positive and negative information. In addition to the universal sign for "no," a picture of

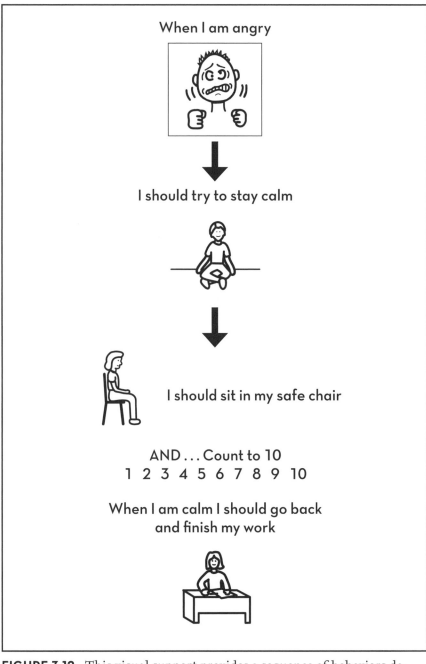

When I am angry

I should try to stay calm

I should sit in my safe chair

AND... Count to 10
1 2 3 4 5 6 7 8 9 10

When I am calm I should go back
and finish my work

FIGURE 3.12. This visual support provides a sequence of behaviors designed for a student to follow when angry. Colors can be used to highlight feelings of anger (red) and calm (green).

FIGURE 3.13. The universal "no" symbol can be placed over an icon representing an off-limit activity, then easily removed.

a stop sign can indicate visually that a behavior is not appropriate. For example, a teacher can place a stop sign on or around his or her desk to remind students that it is not appropriate to play with objects on it.

Some children may need additional visual information to assist them in determining when an activity is an option. A green symbol can indicate "yes" or "go" and be placed on the back of a "no" symbol or stop sign. When it is appropriate for a student to use the material, the "no" symbol can be turned around so that the green "go" or "yes" side of the visual shows. For example, a teacher may place a stop sign on a door to indicate that it is not permissible to leave the room, then turn the sign to a green "go" when the class may exit.

Transition Supports

Transitioning from one activity to another can be confusing for students with ASD. Transitions can be complex in that they require a student to stop a current activity, move to the location of the next activity, and then start another activity. Sometimes the lack of structure to support transitions may prevent students from understanding the steps in a transition or from pre-

No Crashing at School

When I play with my friends,
I should keep my **hands,** my **feet,**
and my **body** to myself.

When I get home I can
crash with my dad.

FIGURE 3.14. This is a visual that pairs negative information (i.e., what not to do) with positive information (i.e., what to do instead).

dicting what will happen next. For other students, resistance to change or their need to cling to rituals and routines may interfere with their ability to successfully transition (Hodgdon, 1995). Still other students may resist transitions because they do not want to leave a preferred item or activity (Frost & Bondy, 2002). All these situations can lead to undesirable or inappropriate behavior. However, visual supports can be implemented to facilitate transitions. The key in developing these supports is to determine which of the previously mentioned factors are affecting the student's ability to transition (Hodgdon, 1995). Visual strategies for transitions can provide students with information that will allow them to better understand their environments, thereby reducing problem behaviors (Hodgdon, 1995). These supports include (a) schedules and transition symbols, (b) time-limit warnings, and (c) transition routines.

Schedules and Transition Symbols

During transition periods, students can carry a picture or object from their daily schedules as destination reminders. If a room is divided and labeled with enlarged symbols, students can match symbols from their daily schedules to those posted in activity areas. At the completion of an activity, a student can place the symbol in a "finished" box or pocket and return to the schedule to determine the next activity. This strategy provides students with transition support while facilitating independence.

Time-Limit Prompts and Warnings

Giving students time-related warnings provides them with a frame of reference. Time-limit prompts and warnings may be paired with auditory or visual cues, such as a bell or timer. Periodically throughout a work period, a teacher may say, "Five minutes left. When the timer sounds, _____ will be finished, and it will be time for _____." For students who need additional support, the verbal cue can be paired with a gesture such as pointing to a timer and manually signing "finished."

When preparing students for the end of an activity that has a natural ending point, such as a game or matching task, teachers should alert students that a transition is approaching by making an appropriate statement or offering an appropriate sign or prompt. For example, a teacher may cue a student by saying, "Only three more words, then spelling will be over" (Hodgdon, 1995).

Transition from Activities with No Definite Ending

Transitions from one activity to another are often very difficult for students with ASD, especially for tasks that have no specific ending point (e.g., swinging, playing with play-dough, using the computer). Visual supports can assist the student in seeing the end to an activity, which helps the student be more independent within the activity, as previously he or she might have relied on verbal prompts to know when to end it (e.g., "One more game on the computer, then you are done," "You can make two more play-dough snakes and then you need to clean up"). For example, if a student is making snakes from play-dough, five photos of play-dough snakes or five sticky notes containing the word "snake" can be placed on the desk. As the student completes each snake, the corresponding icon or sticky note is removed until the student has made five snakes and all five visuals are removed. To enhance this process, a symbol representing "finished" or "check your schedule" can be placed after the last snake symbol to assist the student in independently transitioning to his or her schedule to determine the next task.

Transition Routines

Making transitions a planned part of a routine can also help students with ASD develop the capacity to be flexible in the face of change. For instance, teaching students to put away materials at the completion of a task can function as a natural cue that one activity is ending and another is beginning. If students are reluctant to leave a preferred activity, teachers should let them know when they will be able to return to it. For example, a teacher might say, "You can finish listening to your tape at break," or, "You can play with the ball again at recess." To facilitate smooth transitions, the teacher should design the daily schedule for a balance between preferred and nonpreferred tasks. Placing preferred activities after nonpreferred tasks encourages students to complete their work to move to a preferred activity. It also may be helpful to keep a picture or icon of the preferred activity near a student, where it can serve as a prompt to complete a nonpreferred task (Hodgdon, 1995).

Activity-Completion Signals

Many students with ASD have difficulty knowing how long an activity will last or when they will be asked to transition to another task. Activity-completion signals, such as "finished" pockets or a "finished" box, can provide support for activity transition. Other activity-completion signals may include setting timers for a specified periods of work time and using countdown markers (numbers or colors). A countdown marker is a visual way to show time remaining in an activity. For example, a teacher could take a strip of Velcro and attach cards numbered 1 through 5. When there are 4 minutes left in an activity, the teacher removes the 5 icon, points to the 4 icon and says, "Four minutes left, then _____ will be finished." When there are 3 minutes remaining in the activity, the teacher removes the 4 icon, points to the 3 icon and says, "Three minutes left, then _____ will be finished." The teacher continues this process until all of the numbers are removed from the strip. When the activity is finished and the 1 has been removed, say, "_____ is over. It is time for _____." For a student who may better understand color, three different colored circles can indicate an upcoming transition. A green circle with the word "go" can be placed on the student's desk at the start of the activity. When there are approximately 2 to 3 minutes left in the activity, a yellow circle containing the words "almost done" can be placed on top of the green circle to indicate that the activity will be ending soon. When it is time to stop the task, a red circle containing the word "done," "finished," or "stop" should be placed on the yellow circle. Depending on the needs and abilities of the student, a verbal

37

statement can be paired with the placement of the colored circles. For example, when placing the yellow circle on a student's desk, a teacher could say, "_____ is almost done." When placing the red circle on the student's desk, the teacher could say, "_____ is all done." Figure 3.15 displays an example of a countdown marker.

Timers are another type of completion signal. Some students may respond well to an auditory cue, such as that provided by a traditional timer, but other students may require visual reminders. The Time Timer is an example of a timer that provides a visual cue about the amount of time remaining in an activity. Some teachers prefer the Time Timer over other timers because it does not use an auditory cue. Figure 3.16 shows this item. The Time Tracker is another timer; this one pairs a visual cue with an auditory cue.

As with other visual strategies, teachers must consider each student's functional level when determining the level of abstraction for a completion signal. For example, instead of writing words such as "almost done" or "all done" on colored circles, a teacher may use symbols to represent these concepts.

Introducing Change

The concept of change is challenging for many students with ASD. Their need for sameness and their "limited comprehension of both verbal and nonverbal communication leaves them unprepared for the continuous changes that are part of our species' lifestyle and culture. Consequently, they rely on the predictability of routines and the preservation of physical order to deal with an otherwise too-unpredictable world" (Schuler, 1995, p. 27). One effective way to introduce change is through the use of visual

FIGURE 3.15. This countdown marker can be used to visually represent the passage of time.

FIGURE 3.16. The Time Timer is an activity completion signal that has only a visual indicator of time completion.

schedules. A change symbol, such as the word "change" or a pictorial representation of change, can replace or augment a symbol for the selected activity. For example, if it is raining and the class will be having recess in the multipurpose room instead of outside, the change symbol could be placed in the time slot usually slated for recess. It is important that students see or participate in the symbol removal and replacement process. When possible, the teacher should discuss what will happen instead of the scheduled activity. Some students may need to visit the location of the new activity or to view the replacement materials while carrying or holding the change symbol. Posting a phrase such as "We usually have …" at the top of the schedule can help the student understand that change is an expected variation in the routine (Gray, 1995). Figure 3.17 presents an example of a schedule containing a change symbol.

FIGURE 3.17. Example of the use of a change symbol to indicate an unexpected variation in the schedule.

First–Then Cards

First–then cards have numerous benefits for students with ASD. First, they provide a visual means of introducing new items, curricula, and other materials in a manner that the student understands. As mentioned previously, many students with ASD rely on structure and routines as a means of dealing with the unpredictable world in which they live. This need for sameness makes change, even the smallest change, difficult to handle. The introduction of anything new constitutes a change and therefore can cause the student with ASD stress and anxiety. A second benefit to first–then cards is that they show the student that if he or she completes the depicted nonpreferred task, he or she can then do the preferred task listed next on the card. First–then cards are thus based on the Premack Principle (e.g., if I finish my math, I can play a game on the computer). Figure 3.18 shows an example of a first–then card.

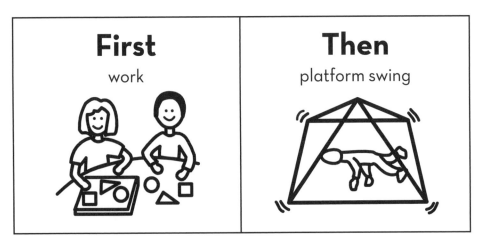

FIGURE 3.18. This first–then card indicates that if the student completes work, he or she will get to swing.

Visual Supports That Structure the Learning Environment

Labels

The physical organization of a classroom can be a crucial element for enhancing success for students. Structure and predictability facilitate students' understanding of environments, thus decreasing the likelihood of stress and agitation. This is particularly important for students with ASD who tend to react negatively to environmental change and uncertainty.

Practices that appear as simple or common as labeling furniture, objects, and the classroom environment can have numerous benefits such as increased independence and decreased anxiety. One place to begin this labeling process is to mark tubs or containers with visual representations of their contents. Visual representations might be miniature objects, icons, or written labels. For example, a teacher would attach a picture of scissors on a tub where scissors are to be placed. Shelves that house common items in the school and classroom environment can also be marked with labels (e.g., homework shelf, math worksheets). Students can then be taught to match labels on containers to labels on shelves, allowing independence in retrieving or returning items to their designated places and decreasing the chances of prompt-led behavioral responses or prompt dependency.

An additional benefit of labeling the classroom is the promotion of language development. For example, if the furniture in a classroom is labeled, students have a visual cue to pair with their teacher's verbal prompt when given requests such as "Sit in chair" or "Stand by door." Labels can also delineate specific areas within a room. For example, enlarged symbols that represent leisure-time activities, reading, or gross-motor skills can be hung above or taped to the area specified for that activity.

Boundary Settings

Boundary markers or boundary settings establish a specific physical space for activities such as playing, reading, or cooking. This visual support helps students differentiate setting expectations while simultaneously providing clear discrimination about where activities can take place. Thus, boundary settings are one more strategy that alleviates the stress and confusion of classroom expectations that many students with ASD experience. Boundary settings are easily incorporated into the existing environment by, for example, sectioning an area on the floor with colored tape or using rugs, carpet remnants, or other materials that indicate where a student is to remain during a given activity (Dalrymple, 1995). If two or more tasks must be completed in the same area or at the same work table, a colored tablecloth, different placemats with visuals of specific behavioral or task expectations, or similar material can distinguish one activity from another. For example, reading could take place with the table uncovered; when it is time for math, a checkered tablecloth could be used to signal the change of activity.

Following Directions

Many students with ASD have difficulty processing auditory information, which poses a major challenge for teachers who need to give instructions and directions (Hodgdon, 1995). Visual strategies such as picture card files, teacher notebooks, and teacher minibooks can help address this challenge. These supports assist students in staying focused long enough to hear the complete set of instructions, to clarify instructions, and to complete the requested tasks (Hodgdon, 1995). Using visual supports will also promote student independence, thereby decreasing the amount of assistance required from teachers.

Picture Card Files

Picture card files graphically depict different tasks to be accomplished during a specific period of time, such as a transition within a given activity. A teacher gives a student a card that specifically directs what he or she should do during a specified time. For example, while completing an art project, the student is asked to get crayons. To support independent completion of this task, the teacher would pull a picture or icon of crayons from the picture card file and give it to the student as a visual tool (Hodgdon, 1995). Figure 5.1 provides an example of a picture card file.

Teacher Notebook

A teacher notebook is a three-ring binder containing pages of visuals that are developed for use during a specific activity. The notebook, open on a table or work area, is designed for use with small groups of students rather than individuals. As the teacher provides instruction or gives directions, he or she can point to the relevant symbols. Pairing the visual with the auditory information creates more effective communication. Oversized visuals can be mounted on poster board for display with larger groups of students (Hodgdon, 1995). Figure 5.2 shows an example of a teacher notebook.

FIGURE 5.1. Example of a picture card file.

Teacher Minibooks

Teacher minibooks are groupings of generic directional pictures and words that students use throughout the day. Direction pictures or icons are placed on separate pages or index cards and inserted into a small photo album or index card notebook. As the teacher gives the student a direction or command, he or she also provides a picture that represents the targeted direction. Teacher minibooks can be divided into different categories or academic areas, which may include pictures for general directions such as "Raise your hand," "Sit in seat," or "Hands in lap." Transition minibooks may contain directions for lining up, waiting in the hallway, being quiet, and so forth (Hodgdon, 1995). Figure 5.3 shows a teacher minibook.

Facilitating Communication Between Environments

An important component of any educational program is effective communication between environments, especially between home and school. There are a variety of visual supports that can enhance such communication.

FIGURE 5.2. A page from a teacher notebook depicts materials used during art.

Visual Bridges

Visual bridges were developed by Hodgdon (1995) as a means of effectively supporting ongoing communication between home and school. One type of visual bridge is the Today at School visual that can be used to assist students in recounting activities that occurred in school. This visual can summarize

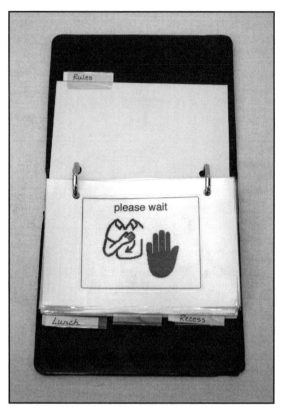

FIGURE 5.3. Example of a teacher minibook.

the entire day or can highlight specific events. Prior to leaving for home, a student can review the day's activities and circle the items on the Today at School visual that were completed. If students have difficulty recalling this information from memory, they can use their visual schedules to guide them. The format of the Today at School visual can vary in accordance with the student's age and abilities (e.g., circling schedule pictures from a page of choices, copying the names of the activities from a visual schedule, completing fill-in-the-blank sentences). Figure 5.4 provides an example of a Today at School visual bridge.

A Last Night at Home visual bridge can serve the same general purpose as the Today at School visual, but in reverse (Hodgdon, 1995). During morning group or during a triage period, teachers can review the information with students. This process can encourage language development and help students understand event sequences.

FIGURE 5.4. "What I Did at School" provides a visual bridge for students.

Remnant Books

Remnant books are another way to facilitate communication between home and school. Remnant books are appropriate for students who require tangible, hands-on support to communicate about past events and are commonly made from cloth placemats, remnants of wallpaper, and plastic baggies. Prior to leaving school, teachers assist students in reviewing their visual schedules and determining what objects to place in the plastic baggies in the remnant book. For example, if a student completed an art project using markers, a marker can be placed in the remnant book to represent this activity. If a student ate grapes for lunch, the grape stem can be placed in the remnant book.

Baggie Books

Baggie books are similar to remnant books in that they provide a more concrete way for students to reference past events. Objects representing activities that occurred during the day can be placed in a baggie labeled "What I did at school today." Figure 5.5 shows a baggie book.

Visual Strategies That Support Social Skill Development

Topic Wheels

Topic wheels are tangible and concrete visual supports that promote conversation on a variety of topics. Such a tool is especially useful with students with ASD because of their common tendency to perseverate on a limited number of topics and unusual obsessive interests. This visual support provides teachers with an opportunity for structured flexibility by giving stu-

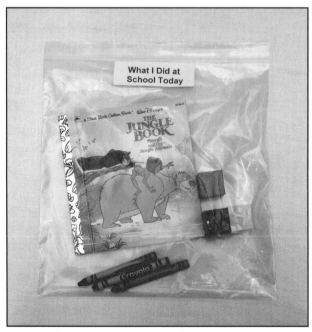

FIGURE 5.5. Example of a baggie book for students who require concrete representations.

dents a random selection of conversation topics from which to choose. An additional strength of this support is its embodiment of choice making. Figure 5.6 provides an example of a topic wheel.

Power Cards

Power cards provide students with ASD visual cues that incorporate their unique special interests, thereby motivating students to practice a desired skill or perform a desired task by linking special interests and adult-identified target responses (Gagnon, 2001). A power card contains a script that links a desired behavior to the student's special interest. For example, a

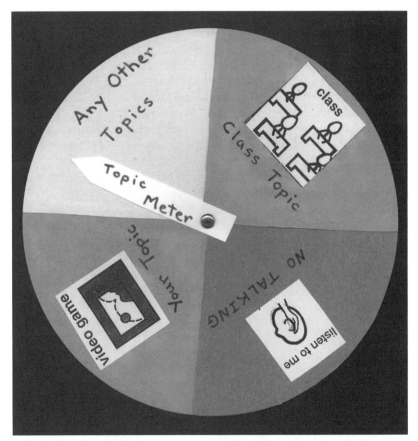

FIGURE 5.6. Topic wheels guide students in appropriate conversation etiquette: Sometimes talking is not allowed, sometimes one can choose the conversation topic, sometimes others choose the topic, and sometimes the topic must relate to the class curriculum.

student with a dominant interest in Spider-Man might be provided a profile and script describing how Spider-Man demonstrates acceptable behavior at school. Thus, school-based role models are created for students based on their unique interests. Similarly, a child with an obsessive interest in vacuum cleaners might be supplied a power card that describes how a Hoover vacuum cleaner salesperson developed specific school-related skills and behaviors to qualify for his sales job. This would be used to motivate the student. When developing the power card script, teachers should compose only two or three sentences written at the student's communication level. A significant advantage of power cards is their size and portability. Because they are approximately the size of a business card, power cards can be easily carried and used in multiple environments. Figure 5.7 shows an example of a power card.

Social Stories

Social story interventions enhance social skill acquisition for many students with ASD. A social story is a minibook that describes a social situation along with appropriate social responses. Social stories are written for individual students and teach specific, desired responses (Gray, 1994) using four sentence types: (a) descriptive sentences, which provide information about subjects, settings, and actions; (b) directive sentences, which describe appropriate behavioral responses; (c) perspective sentences, which identify possible feelings and reactions of others; and (d) affirmative sentences, which can express a commonly held opinion or value.

It is customary for a social story to contain two to five descriptive, perspective, or control sentences for every directive sentence (Gray & Garand, 1993; Swaggart et al., 1995). Social stories for lower functioning students

I want to be strong. I want to wear my Live**Strong** wristband. To be strong like my hero Lance Armstrong, I need to exercise and not just watch TV after school. Even if I don't feel like exercising, I need to. Lance Armstrong says, "Be strong and ride my bike or go on walks after school."

Photo used with permission.

FIGURE 5.7. Example of a power card for a student who likes Lance Armstrong.

may incorporate pictures or icons. Figure 5.8 shows a sample social story for a lower functioning student.

Swaggart et al. (1995) proposed a 10-step process for creating a social story, which involved all aspects of the social story, from identifying a target behavior for change through evaluating the intervention. A brief description of this 10-step process follows.

1. *Identify a target behavior or problem situation.* Begin by selecting a social behavior that may result in increased positive interaction or a learning opportunity for the student. Task-analyze the behavior, breaking it into small, sequential steps. The task analysis should consider the student's strengths.

2. *Define the target behavior for data collection.* Describe a target behavior clearly and concisely. That is, the description should be written so that anyone reading it could identify the desired

---

Playing Games at Recess

I like recess. Recess is fun because I get to swing, play on the slide, and run.

Sometimes I like to play games at recess. My favorite games are tag and soccer.

Sometimes my friends like to play games too. Sometimes my friends like to play my favorite games and sometimes my friends like to play other fun games like football and kickball.

When I want my friends to play tag or soccer, I can walk up to a friend and say "Do you want to play _____?" My friend will either say "Yes" or "No."

If my friends say "Yes" then we can play the game. If my friend says "No" then I can ask him to play another game.

Sometimes my friends won't want to play the same game that I want to play. If my friend doesn't want to play tag or soccer that's O.K.

If my friend doesn't want to play my game I can ...

1. Ask to play his game by saying "Can I play your game?"

2. Ask another person to play a game.

3. Swing, slide, or run

I like recess. I can have fun with my friends when we are playing one of my favorite games or one of their games.

FIGURE 5.8. Social story about recess time designed for a lower functioning student.

behavior. The student involved in the social story must be able to easily recognize the desired behavior.

3. *Collect baseline data on the target behavior.* Prior to intervention, a target behavior should be measured for 3 to 5 days. This allows a teacher to recognize how frequently a behavior is occurring and provides for comparison after the social story has been implemented. Examples of methods for measuring target behavior include placing tally marks on a sheet of paper each time a behavior occurs or using a stopwatch to record the length of time a behavior occurs.

4. *Write a short social story using the four sentence types.* Social stories should be written in the first person, using the aforementioned sentence types. The story can describe either a present situation or a social situation that will occur in the future. Vocabulary and print size correspond with students' developmental and skill levels.

5. *Present one sentence to three sentences on each page.* The format of a social story should be simple to allow a student to focus on and process information associated with each specific element. Presentation of the social story will depend on the needs and skills of individual students. For some students, presenting more than one sentence per page may result in information overload. For others, several sentences on each page may work well.

6. *Use photographs, hand-drawn pictures, or icons.* For students with limited reading skills, the addition of a photograph, picture, or icon to a social story may enhance its understanding. The illustration should not define the described social situation too narrowly, however, because this could result in limited generalization (Gray, 1994).

7. *Read the social story to the student and model the desired behavior.* This step in the social story intervention should become a consistent part of a student's daily schedule. Present the social story several times throughout the day, specifically prior to activities targeted by the story. Students who read independently may share their social story with peers. Nonreading students can follow along or listen as the teacher reads the story.

8. *Collect intervention data.* Using the same procedure as described for baseline data collection, record the occurrence of the target behavior throughout the intervention process. Compare intervention data to baseline data to determine if the social has positively affected the student's social skill development. Teachers should not rely exclusively on memory or anecdotal records to assess the effectiveness of a social story.

9. *Review the findings and related social story procedures.* Use the social story for a minimum of 2 weeks before determining if it

is producing the desired behavior. If the story or program must be altered, change one variable at a time. For example, if a teacher replaces one sentence in the story, he or she should not simultaneously change the time the story is presented or the person who reads it. By changing only one factor at a time it is easier to determine which factors are affecting the student's skill acquisition.

10. *Plan for maintenance and generalization.* Remember that many students with ASD have difficulty maintaining or generalizing skills they have learned. Teachers may ultimately want to fade a social story, but before doing so, they should plan activities to assist the student in generalizing the social story across persons, environments, and situations.

Visual Strategies That Support Calendar and Other Morning Group Activities

Visual strategies can be used to support a variety of classroom activities such as calendar or morning group by assisting students in understanding which students are present and which are absent and concepts such as yesterday, today, and tomorrow, numbers and counting, weather, and classroom jobs. Supports also can visually represent lyrics of common songs or rhythms. Figures 5.9 through 5.11 provide examples of visual supports that can be used during calendar or other morning group activities.

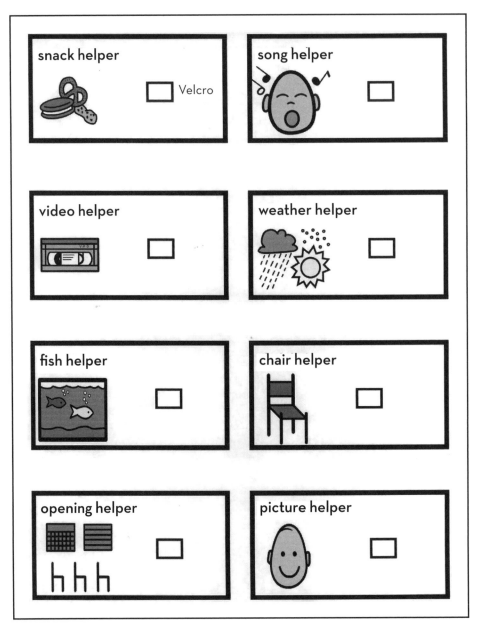

FIGURE 5.9. Pictures or names of students can be attached with Velcro to this visual support that depicts classroom helpers.

FIGURE 5.10. This visual supports activities related to weather and appropriate clothing.

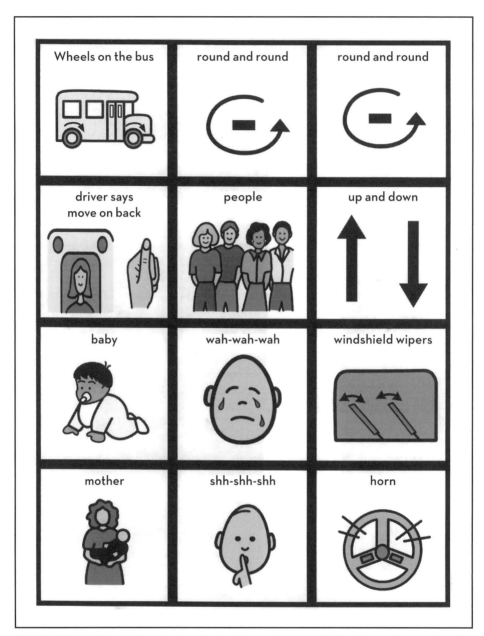

FIGURE 5.11. Visual that depicts lyrics from the song "Wheels on the Bus," to be displayed during the singing of the song.

Conclusion

Visual supports and strategies are effective for students with autism spectrum disorders because the supports rely on students' visual strengths, thus reducing the amount of social and environmental information that may be misunderstood, as compared to verbal communication. Furthermore, visual supports and strategies are simple to create and use and can assist and empower students across multiple settings and situations. Finally, visual supports and strategies can be successfully applied across an individual's lifetime. Indeed, implementation of a variety of visual supports, when paired with other interventions, can assist in creating a successful learning environment for students with autism spectrum disorders.

References

Carr, E. (1985). Behavioral approaches to communication in autism. In E. Schopler & G. Mesibov (Eds.), *Communication problems in autism*. New York: Plenum Press.

Dalrymple, N. J. (1995). Environmental supports to develop flexibility and independence. In K. A. Quill (Ed.), *Teaching children with autism: Strategies to enhance communication and socialization*. New York: Delmar.

Downing, J. E., & Peckham-Hardin, K. D. (2001). Daily schedules: A helpful learning tool. *Teaching Exceptional Children, 33*(3), 62–68.

Frost, L., & Bondy, A. (2002). *The Picture Exchange Communication System training manual* (2nd ed). Newark, DE: Pyramid Educational Products.

Gagnon, E. (2001). *Power cards: Using special interests to motivate children and youth with Asperger syndrome and autism*. Shawnee Mission, KS: Autism Asperger.

Grandin, T. (1995). *Thinking in Pictures: And other reports from my life with autism*. New York: Vintage Books.

Gray, C. (1994). *Comic strip conversations: Colorful, illustrated interactions with students with autism and related disorders*. Jenison, MI: Jenison Public Schools.

Gray, C. (1995). *Social stories unlimited: Social stories and comic strip conversations*. Jenison, MI: Jenison Public Schools.

Gray, C., & Garand, J. D. (1993). Social stories: Improving responses of students with autism with accurate social information. *Focus on Autistic Behavior, 8*, 1–10.

Hodgdon, L. A. (1995). *Visual strategies for improving communication: Practical supports for school and home*. Troy, MI: QuirkRoberts.

Hodgdon, L. A. (1999). *Solving behavior problems in autism: Improving communication with visual strategies*. Troy, MI: QuirkRoberts.

MacDuff, G. S., Krantz, P. J., & McClannahan, L. E. (1993). Teaching children with autism to use photographic activity schedules: Maintenance and generalization of complex response chains. *Journal of Applied Behavior Analysis, 26*, 89–97.

Quill, K. A. (1995). *Teaching children with autism: Strategies to enhance communication and socialization*. New York: Delmar.

Savner, J. L., & Myles, B. S. (2000). *Making visual supports work in the home and community: Strategies for individuals with autism and Asperger syndrome*. Shawnee Mission, KS: Autism Asperger.

Schuler, A. L. (1995). Thinking in autism: Differences in learning and development. In K. A. Quill (Ed.), *Teaching children with autism: Strategies to enhance communication and socialization*. New York: Delmar.

Swaggart, B., Gagnon, E., Bock, S., Earles, T., Quinn, C., Myles, B. S., & Simpson, R. (1995). Using social stories to teach social and behavioral skills to children with autism. *Focus on Autistic Behavior, 10*, 1–6.

Twachtman, D. (1995). Methods to enhance communication in verbal children. In K. A. Quill (Ed.), *Teaching children with autism: Strategies to enhance communication and socialization.* New York: Delmar.

Williams, D. (1994). *Somebody somewhere.* New York: Times Books.

Richard L. Simpson, PhD, is professor of special education at the University of Kansas. He currently directs several federally supported projects to prepare teachers and other leaders for careers with children and youth with autism spectrum disorders. Simpson has also worked as a teacher of students with disabilities, a psychologist, and an administrator of several programs for students with autism. He is the former editor of the journal *Focus on Autism and Other Developmental Disabilities* and the author of numerous books and articles on autism spectrum disorders.

Theresa L. Earles-Vollrath, PhD, is an assistant professor of special education at Central Missouri State University. Earles-Vollrath received her doctorate degree from the University of Kansas with an emphasis in autism and behavior disorders. She previously worked as a teacher for children with autism, as the director of the Autism Resource Center located at the University of Kansas Medical Center, and as an autism specialist for a public school district. In addition to teaching at the college level, Earles-Vollrath also serves as a consultant to school districts.

Katherine Tapscott Cook, PhD, is assistant professor of education at Missouri Western State University. Cook has worked in the field of special education for the past 15 years as an educator and an educational consultant for parents and school districts. Cook's principal research interests include sensory dysfunction and social communication deficits in students with autism spectrum disorders.

Jennifer B. Ganz, PhD, is assistant professor of special education at the University of Texas at San Antonio. In addition, Ganz has experience as a general and special education teacher, an educational consultant, and a respite-care volunteer, and has presented lectures and workshops on social, communication, and behavioral interventions. Ganz's research involves improving social and communication skills in individuals with autism spectrum disorders and developmental disabilities.